The Arms Trade

ADAM HIBBERT

FRANKLIN WATTS
LONDON • SYDNEY

First published in 2003 by Franklin Watts
96 Leonard Street, London EC2A 4XD

Franklin Watts Australia
45–51 Huntley Street
Alexandria, NSW 2015

Copyright © Franklin Watts 2003
Series editor: Rachel Cooke
Editor: Andrew Campbell
Series design: White Design
Picture research: Diana Morris

A CIP catalogue record for this book is available from the British Library.

ISBN: 0 7496 4887 2

Printed in Belgium

Acknowledgements:
Action Press/Rex Features: 13. Dimitri Beliakov/Rex Features: 20. Benelux/Zefa: 18b. Adrian Brooks/Rex Features: 23t.
Corrine Dufka/Reuters/Popperfoto: front cover and 15. EPA/PA Photos: 8, 29t. Alain Haas/Sipa/Rex Features: 21t.
Tom Heneghan/Reuters/Popperfoto: 5. Ho/Reuters/Popperfoto: 25t. Chris Ison/PA Photos: 12b.
Isopress Senepont/Rex Features: 4c. Saheed Khan/AFP/Popperfoto: 26–27t. Colin King: 27b.
John Kuntz/Reuters/Popperfoto: 21b. Jean-Pierre Laffont/Corbis Sygma: 28. Manoocher/Sipa/Rex Features: 25c.
Peter Morgan/Reuters/Popperfoto: 24. Peter Mueller/Reuters/Popperfoto: 14. Alain Nogues/Corbis Sygma: 4t.
Novosti/Sipa/Rex Features: 7. PA Photos: 29b. Robert Patrick/Corbis Sygma: 19. Popperfoto: 6t, 6b, 17t.
Neil Rabinowitz/Corbis: 9. Rex Features: 10, 12t, 26b. Fatih Saribas/Reuters/Popperfoto: 18t. Sipa/Rex Features: 11.
Trippett/Sipa/Rex Features: 17b. Arthur Tsang/Reuters/Bettmann/Popperfoto: 23b.
J. Widdowson/TRH Pictures: 16. Zada/Sipa/Rex Features: 22.

The publisher would like to acknowledge the Stockholm International Peace Research Institute (SIPRI)
as the source of much of the information in this book.

Data on the UK economy (page 19) by permission of the Institute for Fiscal Studies.

Whilst every attempt has been made to clear copyright, should there be any inadvertent
omission please apply in the first instance to the publisher regarding rectification.

CONTENTS

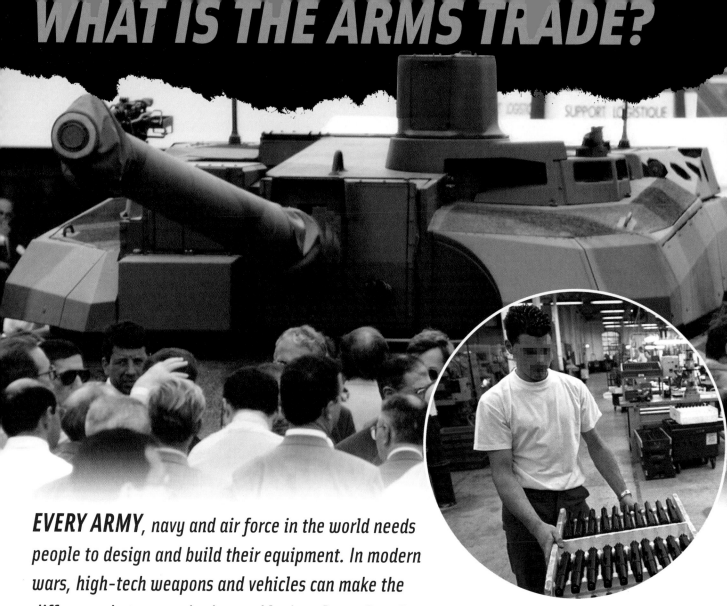

WHAT IS THE ARMS TRADE?

EVERY ARMY, *navy and air force in the world needs people to design and build their equipment. In modern wars, high-tech weapons and vehicles can make the difference between winning and losing. But only a few countries and companies have the technology needed to make up-to-date equipment. This means that armed forces often have to buy their supplies on the international market.*

↑ *Making weapons and other military supplies is a profitable industry which provides thousands of jobs.*

↖ *A tank on display to shoppers at an arms market or 'arms fair'.*

THE ARMS MAKERS

Arms manufacturers exist all over the globe, but the biggest belong to some of the leading economies of the world: the USA, France, the UK, China and Russia. US companies account for almost half the world arms trade each year. As more countries develop their industries, new arms suppliers appear – Israel, Turkey and South Korea are important new suppliers.

GOODS AND SERVICES

The arms trade is not simply about making a weapon and selling it – the market includes vehicles, uniforms, computer systems and other electronic equipment. Services are also bought and sold, from maintaining and customising (adapting) weapons to military training and even the hire of professional soldiers, called mercenaries.

GET THE FACTS STRAIGHT

This table shows leading countries' sales and spending on arms (in US$).

Top 10 arms sellers	Exports ($million)	Top 10 arms buyers	Imports ($million)	Top 10 military budgets	Total spent ($million)	Per citizen ($)
USA	33,000	Saudi Arabia	7,700	USA	290,000	1,200
UK	5,200	Turkey	3,200	Russia	45,000	310
Russia	3,100	Japan	3,000	France	40,000	800
France	2,900	Taiwan	2,600	Japan	39,000	350
Germany	1,900	UK	2,600	UK	37,000	600
Sweden	670	Israel	2,400	Germany	33,000	500
Israel	600	South Korea	2,200	China	27,000	20
Australia	550	Greece	1,900	Saudi Arabia	26,000	1,400
Canada	550	USA	1,600	Italy	25,000	400
Ukraine	550	Germany	1,300	Brazil	15,000	90

Source: US State Department figures for 1999 and other estimates, averaged over 1998–2001.

These Afghan fighters use old rifles, sold by the British army when it upgraded to more modern guns.

OFFICIAL AND UNOFFICIAL

Most arms makers sell to their own governments, and to others around the world that they are allowed to trade with by their governments. Some trading is done by governments themselves, selling off surplus or old-fashioned equipment to another nation. But there is also an illegal arms trade, supplying weapons to people or governments by secretive methods.

ARMS IN THE NEWS

The arms trade is big business. In 2001, the United Nations estimated that $840 billion was spent on the military – 2.6% of all global production. The arms trade is also a controversial business because it sells tools for making war. Some people argue that the arms trade even causes wars. Others say that it stops war, by allowing more people to defend themselves. Whatever its effect, war or the threat of war keeps the arms trade in the news.

IN THE 19TH CENTURY, industrial manufacture and new technology began to give certain countries a huge advantage in warfare. Arms makers made fortunes supplying the world's leading armies with new inventions, from machine guns to submarines.

DO-IT-YOURSELF

In the 20th century, the arms trade was changed by the need for nations to have their own factories and abilities to make military equipment. During the First World War (1914–1918), countries on both sides of the conflict were able to disrupt each other's supply of arms from outside their borders. To be sure of surviving another war, countries bought new technology and built up their own arms industries. This is called creating a 'Defence Industrial Base'.

↗ The Swedish inventor Alfred Nobel (1833–1896) made a fortune from his inventions, including an explosive used to shoot bullets out of guns. He used much of his money to establish the Nobel prizes, including a prize for peace.

THE COLD WAR

After the Second World War (1939–1945), the Western powers and the Soviet Union competed for influence over world resources, such as oil fields. Both sides offered arms to countries with those resources, in order to build alliances. In addition, the USA and the Soviet Union (the two world superpowers) smuggled weapons to rebels in countries whose governments supported the opposing superpower. This era of tension without direct conflict is known as the Cold War.

⬇ One of the German U-boats that sank many British ships during the First World War. This tactic interrupted Britain's supply of arms from other countries.

→ *Russian troops parade in Moscow. Parades symbolised the Soviet Union's military power during the Cold War.*

A NEW ERA

With the collapse of the Soviet Union and the end of the Cold War in 1991, global military spending fell by about one third. Most of this reduction came from Russia, where defence spending fell from $257 billion in 1987 to $24 billion in 1997. Arms firms, especially in Eastern Europe, faced ruin unless they could sell their products to new markets, such as Africa and the Middle East.

THE MIDDLE EAST AND TERROR

Arms spending increased again at the start of the 21st century, as tension in the Middle East and the US 'War on Terror' put military security back in the headlines. In the 12 months following September 11th 2001, the share value of arms makers such as Lockheed Martin and Raytheon rose by between 39 and 66 per cent.

WHAT DO YOU THINK?

Most of us would prefer to use technology and skilled workers on projects that help humanity. But governments are responsible for national security, and have to consider what resources they need to defend their countries from attack. As a result, governments buy weapons from arms companies even when there is no immediate need to use them.

● Do you think governments should spend taxpayers' money on arms?

● What other areas, if any, do you think this money could be spent on?

BUYING AND SELLING ARMS normally takes place quietly, in hotel rooms or embassies. But every year, arms companies put on arms fairs and airshows all around the world. These events are the 'shop window' of the arms trade. They allow buyers to inspect the latest equipment, meet suppliers and discuss their needs. The important stages in many arms deals happen at these fairs.

BATTLE-TESTED

High-tech weapons are difficult to make and are sometimes unreliable on the battlefield. However, when a weapon has been shown to work in an actual war, an arms company can say that the product is 'battle-tested' – a big advantage over its untested rivals. For example, at the Asian Aerospace airshow in 2002, Unmanned Aerial Vehicles (UAVs) proved popular after their successful use by the US Army against the Taliban regime in Afghanistan. UAVs are remote-controlled aircraft that can carry loads such as missiles, cameras or sensors.

ENTERTAINING THE CROWDS

Unlike arms fairs, airshows are normally open to the public. Warplane makers from several countries put on displays to entertain crowds, and buyers meet businessmen in the quieter spots. Warplanes are too expensive for most arms firms to keep demonstration models for use in airshows. Instead, manufacturers usually borrow aircraft from governments that have recently bought them.

MILITARY SUPPORT

Military staff often attend arms fairs and airshows to demonstrate products from their countries. They may simply discuss what a weapons system can do for a customer, or they may perform mock battles to show how equipment works in practice. Some campaigners argue that military staff should not be used as salesmen for arms companies, since they are employed by taxpayers to defend their own country (see page 25).

→ A group of European arms makers built this Eagle 1 UAV (Unmanned Aerial Vehicle), on sale at a French airshow in Paris in 2001.

GET THE FACTS STRAIGHT

The world's top 10 arms companies

Rank	Name	Country	Leading products	Annual sales ($ billion)
1	Lockheed Martin	USA	aircraft, systems	18.6
2	Boeing	USA	jets, helicopters, missiles	16.9
3	BAe Systems	UK	jets, ships, bullets	14.4
4	Raytheon	USA	missiles, systems	10.1
5	Northrop Grumman	USA	aircraft, ships, systems	6.6
6	General Dynamics	USA	ships, armoured vehicles, IT	6.5
7	EADS	France, Germany, Spain	missiles, jets	5.3
8	Thales	France	defence electronics, systems	5.1
9	Litton	USA	electronics, IT, naval systems	3.9
10	TRW	USA	defence electronics, systems	3.3

'Systems' include computer equipment, radars and missile guidance systems.
Since 2000, Northrop Grumman has bought both Litton and TRW.
Source: Stockholm International Peace Research Institute (SIPRI) Yearbook, 2000.

⬆ Families attend Abbotsford Airshow, Canada. This show is not for the trade, but does 'market' bombers and fighters to around 150,000 tourists each year.

Brazil took on ownership of the Admiral Foch aircraft carrier in 2000, in a deal worth nearly $100 million to France.

AROUND 90 PER CENT of the money made through arms sales is official, with proper documentation and reports to the United Nations (see page 24). But this high percentage is caused by a small number of billion-dollar deals for equipment such as aircraft, ships or tanks. Several thousand illegal arms deals are made each year for small arms, such as guns and explosives. Trade in these goods is hugely profitable.

AN OFFICIAL DEAL

In November 2000, France sold the 37-year-old aircraft carrier *Admiral Foch* to Brazil, in a typical deal. France wanted to modernise its navy and could no longer use the ship, but it was worth very little on the second-hand market. Brazil paid a bargain price of $12 million. But this low price went with an agreement to buy new French-built jets and other equipment to the value of $80 million. The deal was declared to the United Nations.

DODGIER DEALS

Trading arms that have not been officially approved is a specialist skill. Traders have to know whom to bribe to be given a false 'end user certificate', a sort of passport for arms shipments that declares which country is buying the arms. Officials in Peru, Jordan and several other countries have been said to issue these false documents in exchange for bribes. Once they have left the country that was selling them, arms can be diverted to illegal destinations.

MASS DESTRUCTION

Some arms are very tightly controlled, particularly Weapons of Mass Destruction (WMDs), which include nuclear, biological and chemical weapons. After the Cold War, there were fears that unemployed scientists in Russia would sell their skills in WMDs to other countries. However, this has not happened, so countries and terrorist networks that want WMDs have had to steal secrets or fund their own research. They may purchase raw materials or technology abroad, but the arms trade is not involved.

FACING THE ISSUES

US journalist Ken Silverstein has spent years investigating the people behind the grey (semi-legal) or black (illegal) market in military equipment. In his book *Private Warriors*, Silverstein describes one trader called Ernst Werner Glatt, who, in the 1970s and 1980s, bought black market weapons from communist countries. On behalf of the USA, Glatt secretly traded these arms to anti-communist rebels that were supported by America in various countries. The USA preferred supplying communist weapons for two reasons. Firstly, they could not be traced back to the US military. Secondly, both the rebels and the armies they fought used the same guns and bullets, so the rebels could win new supplies on the battlefield. Glatt's deals made him a fortune. He owned estates in the USA, Scotland and Austria, as well as three Swiss chalets and a flat in London.

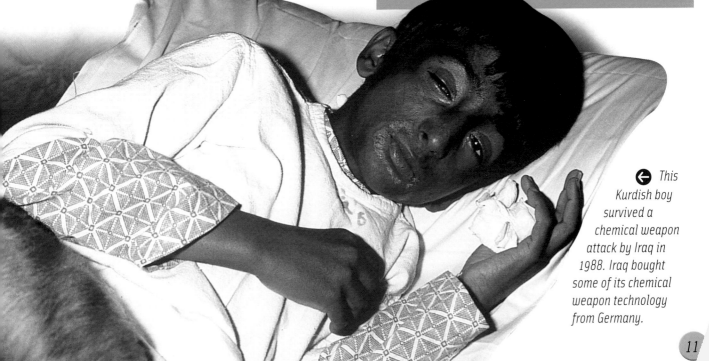

This Kurdish boy survived a chemical weapon attack by Iraq in 1988. Iraq bought some of its chemical weapon technology from Germany.

AT THE END of the Cold War, many countries reduced the size of their armies. Between 1987 and 1994, roughly five million soldiers lost their jobs. Most of them learned new skills and joined the normal economy. But thousands carried on working as soldiers for private military companies (PMCs). Soldiers offered for hire are called mercenaries. Mercenaries might be involved in training regular soldiers or fighting battles.

In the 1980s US advisers taught tank skills to Iraqi soldiers. These skills were vital for Iraq's war with Iran.

PAYING FOR PEACE

PMCs offer soldiers for hire to international bodies such as the United Nations (UN), as well as to countries and other groups. The UN force that served in Yugoslavia in the mid-1990s included soldiers provided by a PMC called DynCorp. The contract with DynCorp became embarrassing when allegations were made that some of its employees were earning extra money by trading in small arms, and even by selling East European women to become prostitutes.

➜ *Kathryn Bolkovac lost her job after reporting illegal activities by other DynCorp employees. She was awarded over £100,000 by a UK court.*

BRIEFCASES AND BULLETS

Western firms working in unstable countries often pay to be protected by a mercenary security force. They may pay the government to hire private soldiers for them. But mercenary forces can be unpopular. In 1997, Papua New Guinea's army almost revolted when the government tried to use mercenaries to recapture a copper mine belonging to the Rio Tinto mining company. The mine was on the island of Bougainville, where armed rebels demanded independence from the government.

TRAINING THE TROOPS

Governments and arms makers can offer military services, such as training. This might be part of an arms deal, so purchasers can learn how to use their new equipment. L-3 Communications is a US company that provides flight simulator training for pilots, as well as weapons training. It works with the US Army and international customers.

← *A member of the private military company MPRI trains soldiers in Croatia. During the war between Croatia and Serbia in the 1990s, the Croatian army was criticised for its treatment of Serbian civilians.*

OBSERVERS AND TRAINERS

Governments can also send military staff as 'observers' to countries they have supplied with arms. The observers may share battle skills and training with the foreign armies. Sometimes these deals are done for money; at other times they are done to help an ally facing a military threat. In 1975, communist Cuba sent thousands of troops to help the socialist government of Angola fight off a force backed by the USA and South Africa.

WHAT DO YOU THINK?

- Do you think there is a difference between selling someone arms and hiring out soldiers to fight a war for them?
- Can you think of any problems that might arise from using hired mercenaries instead of regular soldiers?
- If mercenaries were banned, some countries would be avoided by big business. What do you think the effects of this might be? Is this a price worth paying?
- What laws should apply to mercenaries? The laws of their home country or the country they are serving in?

THOSE IN FAVOUR of the arms trade argue that if all sides are well-armed, nobody will gain from going to war. Other people argue that wars are encouraged by the supply of arms. Since the end of the Cold War, the United Nations has had to cope with more civil wars than ever before. The break-up of Yugoslavia in the early 1990s was just one example.

POLICING PEACE

As the only surviving superpower, the USA has found its military resources stretched to cover all the United Nations' peacekeeping projects. America's position provides an argument for the arms trade – other countries should arm themselves to help enforce peace around the world. In practice, countries that do not send troops abroad pay others to do so. In 1991, Germany gave roughly $7.5 billion to the USA to help pay for the Gulf War in Iraq.

→ German troops and tanks in Kosovo, Yugoslavia, in 1999. Eight years after the Gulf War, Germany participated in the international peacekeeping mission in Kosovo.

GET THE FACTS STRAIGHT

Civil wars usually rely on armies and militia groups having access to small arms.

- Small arms include pistols, rifles, machine guns and small explosives, such as mines, grenades and rockets.

- The percentage of war casualties who were civilians has risen from around 5 per cent at the beginning of the 20th century to roughly 80 per cent by the year 2000. Small arms account for many of these deaths.

- Small arms can be used to take over small countries. A coup in Liberia in 1990 used money taken from the diamond trade to buy small arms. About 150,000 people died in the civil war. In 1999, after the war had ended, 25,000 guns were destroyed in a ceremony to signal Liberia's return to peace.

↑ Without free access to cheap arms in Liberia, these children could not have been kidnapped and used as soldiers in the 1990s.

ARMS RACES

Whenever a country buys arms to improve its strength in a region, its neighbours are forced to spend more to maintain a balance. But once those neighbours have improved their weapons, the first country finds it has to spend more to regain its lead. This is called an arms race. In such situations, governments usually divert funds to military spending and the military becomes more powerful, which can threaten democracy. At the beginning of the 21st century there are arms races in the Middle East, central Africa, the Indian subcontinent and South-east Asia. In all these regions money is badly needed for social development, for example spending on health care and education.

WAR MONGERING?

In 1934, the US Senate set up the Nye Commission to investigate the role of arms makers in promoting war. The report decided that arms salesmen 'produce fear, hostility and greater munitions orders on the part of neighbouring countries, [leading to] economic strain and collapse or war'. The report led to the creation of the Office of Munitions Control, which until 1990 limited US arms exports. Governments today constantly review what controls to put on their arms manufacturers.

SELF-DEFENCE

ARTICLE 51 *of the United Nations' charter says that every country has a right to 'self-determination', in other words to make free political choices about who rules it and what goals to aim for. But some countries may still be bullied by their neighbours. A well-armed defence force can give a country some safety from others. So the arms trade can be seen as helping to defend the rights laid out in Article 51.*

FINDING A BALANCE

A balance of power exists between countries when neither side can be sure of winning a fight against the other. At the start of the Cold War, for example, only the USA had the ability to drop nuclear bombs anywhere in the world. The Soviet Union copied American technology from a captured US bomber, and built its own bomber force. The restored balance in arms technology may have helped to keep the peace.

WHAT DO YOU THINK?

- Should every country have the right to defend itself? If not, who should decide?
- Can you think of situations when it might be OK to sell arms to rebel armies?
- If you had to decide to sell arms to a rebel army, what would you care most about: the views of the rebels, the regime they were rebelling against, your own country's interests or international law?
- Do countries with strong defence forces help to keep the world peaceful?
- If you were in charge of a poor country, how would you feel about rich countries telling you not to buy arms?

The Tupolev TU-4 bomber plane, known as the Flying Fortress, was built by the Soviet Union from designs based on a captured American plane, the B-29 Superfort.

CIVIL WAR

There is another aspect to self-defence. Citizens sometimes choose governments that are then threatened by military coups, or revolts, and may try to arm themselves to defend their choice. In the Spanish Civil War (1936–39), a military coup against the Republican government was supported by both Germany and Italy. The German arms dealer Admiral Wilhelm Canaris tried to prevent Spanish Republicans from defending their government: he sold them guns and bullets that were useless.

ARMING REBELS

While the arms trade is important to national self-defence it can also undermine it, by supplying rebel groups with weapons. Most countries say that they ban the sale of weapons to rebels. But between 10 and 20 per cent of all arms sold end up in the hands of rebel groups. In the 1980s, the USA secretly supplied tons of small arms to anti-communist rebels in Afghanistan and Nicaragua.

⬆ *Spanish civilians tried to defend their government from a military coup in the 1930s, but struggled with poor equipment. In contrast, the military used sophisticated German weapons.*

BUYING ON CREDIT

The United Nations Development Programme says that the arms trade undermines self-defence in another way. Poor countries often buy their weapons 'on credit', which has to be paid back over a period of years. This may cause poverty and instability, which can lead to civil war.

➡ *US Army Colonel Oliver North was exposed in 1989 for using arms traders to supply weapons to rebels in Nicaragua.*

ARMS AND THE ECONOMY

← This Turkish F-16 Fighting Falcon is an American design, but was built in a Turkish factory as part of an offset deal.

MANY PEOPLE BELIEVE that the arms trade boosts countries' economies. They say that it develops industry, provides jobs and raises a nation's level of exports. But critics argue that the arms trade has only a limited impact on jobs or exports. They also suggest that poor nations that spend money on arms have little money left over for social and economic development.

PROTECTION FROM COMPETITION

Domestic production of arms can be very important to a nation's security (see page 6). For this reason, the World Trade Organisation (WTO) allows countries to protect their own arms industries from foreign competition – something WTO members cannot normally do with other industries. The WTO also allows countries to favour their own arms makers by giving them extra money, called subsidies.

DEVELOPING INDUSTRIES

Large arms deals can also allow buyers to develop their own country's economy. In return for buying arms, 'offset' deals agree that some of the equipment is built in the buyer's country. In 1983, Turkey bought 156 F-16 fighter-bombers from the USA. As part of the deal, 148 of the planes were built in Turkey by a Turkish company. Offset deals do not help employment in the seller's country, but give developing countries a way to develop their industries.

← In one offset deal in 1996, the USA sold Thailand war jets in exchange for a variety of goods, including chickens. The chickens were then sold in the USA.

FACING THE ISSUES

In 2000, the British Ministry of Defence paid for research to study the cost to the UK economy of cutting defence exports by half. The report found that there would be a one-off cost of around £1 billion, and a yearly cost of less than £100 million (about 0.3 per cent of annual UK defence spending). The report found that the demand for skilled defence workers in other industries would lead to an overall gain in the number of jobs. In summary, the experts said that the economic case for the arms trade is not significant.

Source: The Economic Costs and Benefits of UK Defence Exports, Fiscal Studies, September 2002.

COSTING AN ARM AND A LEG

The end of the Cold War meant, in theory, that countries could spend less on arms and more on social projects, such as healthcare and housing. However, an increase in regional conflicts in the 1990s meant that few governments cut their military spending. Poor countries that buy arms to defend themselves have little money left over for social needs. Angola and Sierra Leone are two poor nations that have passed on income from their natural resources (oil and diamonds) to buy arms.

SWORDS INTO PLOUGHSHARES

Peace campaigners try to persuade arms companies to use their factories and workers to make consumer goods. But because arms makers are accustomed to government subsidies, they often need a lot of help to produce non-military goods and sell them in a highly competitive market. The Petrovsky arms factory in Nizhny, Russia, has been helped by the electronics company Samsung to make car stereos instead of weapons.

⊙ Despite owning some of the world's best diamond mines, Sierra Leone has experienced severe development problems as a result of civil war.

DIPLOMACY IS THE WORK *of governments dealing with other governments. Diplomats have to think hard about how their decisions affect other countries. For example, a Western country that sells arms to Israel risks offending other countries in the Middle East, such as Syria or Yemen. These countries might regard the sale as an indication of support for the Israelis in their conflict with the Palestinians.*

The deal for the Admiral Gorshkov involved Russia 'giving' the carrier to India. In return, India paid a Russian shipyard millions of dollars to modernise the 1980s' ship.

BUILDING FRIENDSHIPS

One big reason for a country to trade arms is to develop friendships with foreign powers. Most weapons systems require training and spare parts to be supplied alongside the hardware itself. Military leaders and businessmen from both countries learn to work together. In 2003, India's negotiations with Russia for the purchase of an aircraft carrier, the *Admiral Gorshkov*, involved an agreement that hundreds of Indian sailors would visit Russia for training.

CLUBBING TOGETHER

Sometimes there is a direct military reason for countries to work together. The North Atlantic Treaty Organisation (NATO) is a group of European and North American countries that work together on defence issues. Arms sales from America to its NATO partners have meant that the allies share compatible equipment, such as missiles and bullets. This makes their alliance more efficient.

THE BOOMERANG EFFECT

One problem with diplomacy based on arms relationships is that allies can suddenly become enemies. This is known as the 'boomerang effect'. In the 1970s, US president Richard Nixon gave America's allies more access to US arms. Between 1970 and 1982, US arms sales rose from $5 billion to $27 billion. But some allies are unpredictable. In 1979, the US-friendly Shah of Iran lost power in an Islamic revolution. Iran's new, anti-American leaders took control of the Shah's US weapons.

→ *Nations sometimes work together on military tasks. This French soldier served with the UN force in Bosnia in the mid-1990s. Buying guns and equipment from the same arms company makes working together easier.*

HOME TO ROOST

The problem of the boomerang effect is that countries such as the USA become trapped in an arms race with themselves. Because it had sold F-16 and F-18 jets to many clients in the Middle East, America faced a real challenge if it embarked upon any military operation there. It had to spend billions of dollars to create a new super-jet, the F-22, to regain the advantage.

↓ *This state-of-the-art F-22 warplane cost $69 billion to design. The US Air Force had to buy it because so many possible enemies around the world own other US warplanes.*

WHAT DO YOU THINK?

● How would you predict which of your allies might become your enemy in the future?

● Can you think of other ways than arms sales to promote stronger links between countries?

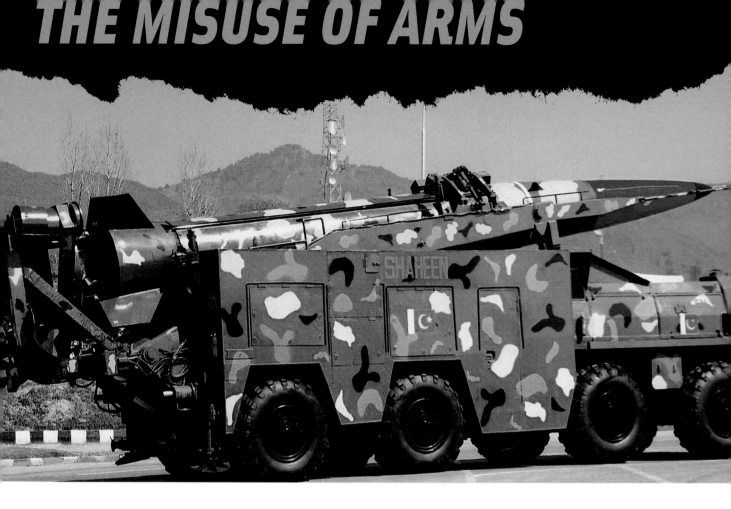

ARMS SALES do not simply give a country the power to defend itself from other countries. Arms can also be used by a government to bully its own citizens. Countries such as the USA, Britain, France and Australia set rules that are meant to stop their arms being supplied to governments that deny human rights to their own citizens. But these rules are easily broken.

RIGHTS AND WRONGS

Part of the problem lies in the definition of rights. When Indonesia invaded East Timor in 1975, the international community could not agree whether this was an abuse of the human rights of the East Timorese. While it debated, countries continued to supply military equipment. At a cemetery in Dili in 1991, the Indonesian regime shot dead 271 peaceful protesters – 382 more were wounded and 250 'disappeared'.

A BUYER'S MARKET

Especially since the end of the Cold War, buyers have been able to 'shop around' for weapons. If one country decides not to supply them, they can find another country that will. It is very difficult to prevent a sale to a regime with a bad record on human rights. Arms-selling countries usually fail to co-operate to stop such sales.

➡ *In 1989, students in China demonstrated for democracy in Tiananmen Square, Beijing, but their demands met with military force. Police used British-supplied CCTV cameras to identify and arrest protesters.*

← A Pakistani Shaheen missile, capable of carrying a nuclear warhead. The dual use of nuclear power – for energy needs as well as war – makes it hard to deny access to the technology.

→ Mohammed al Mas'ari, a political refugee from Saudi Arabia. In 1996 the UK government tried to expel him – many believe that this was to avoid offending a major purchaser of UK arms.

DUAL USE

Some security equipment may seem harmless, but it can be used in human rights abuses. In the mid-1980s, a British CCTV system was installed in Beijing, China, to help police with traffic jams. In 1989, the cameras were used to identify and arrest protesters who were demanding democracy. Some countries have also acquired materials for making Weapons of Mass Destruction by claiming they need the imports – such as chemicals or nuclear equipment – for non-military purposes.

PROBLEMS WITH DEMOCRACY

In democracies, government officials are meant to serve the voters. However, the secrecy of arms sales makes it possible for officials to be bribed. In 1999, Bangladesh bought eight Mig-29 jets from Russia for $120 million, almost double the price expected. The purchase went against the advice of many elected politicians, who could see that it was against the best interests of the voters. There are strong suspicions that bribery was involved in the deal.

REGULATING ARMS

THE UNITED NATIONS *keeps a Register of Conventional Weapons, updated annually with information freely supplied by its 191 members. Good information helps neighbouring countries avoid being tricked into costly arms races by arms traders. But the register cannot help with arms sales that a government prefers to hide, and only covers big weapons and vehicles – not small arms such as guns, mines or small missiles.*

⬇ *Countries meet at the United Nations to agree rules about the arms trade. The five permanent members of the UN Security Council are among the world's top ten arms producers.*

FROM SMALL ARMS TO MISSILES

It is hard to control small arms because so many countries can make them. In the late 1990s, the UK stopped several arms sales to Indonesia, because of tensions after East Timor voted in favour of independence (see page 22). Yet Indonesia still bought 1,000 H&K machine guns. The British-owned H&K company had licensed a Turkish firm to make the guns, which it sold to Indonesia. UK law could not stop this.

Some weapons are covered by 'non-proliferation' agreements – banning the sale of high-tech weapons to countries that do not already have them. Weapons of Mass Destruction are covered by such agreements, as well as some missile technology. Some people argue that this approach prevents developing nations becoming the equals of richer countries.

The ex-president of Costa Rica, Oscar Arias. Many international campaigns support his idea that all nations should promise to stop supplying weapons to unstable or abusive countries.

↑ In December 2002, Spanish marines searched this ship, the So San, and found 15 North Korean SCUD missiles. Inspections like this can prevent illegal arms trading.

CODES OF CONDUCT

Countries may agree to codes of conduct, such as the International Code of Conduct on Arms Transfers, launched by Oscar Arias, the ex-president of Costa Rica. The code contains a checklist that forbids nations to sell weapons to governments that do not respect human rights, peace and democracy. But defining what is a weapon can be difficult. For example, the UK will not sell guns to China, but does sell laser sights for guns.

DOMESTIC POLITICS

Small steps can be taken by politicians to restrain their own country's arms trade. In 1993, the US Congress put limits on military personnel giving free help to US arms firms at arms fairs. The limit required the President to give Congress 45 days' notice of such events. However, by the late 1990s the arms trade was still taking around $30 million each year in free help from the military, and Congress began to consider tougher restrictions.

GET THE FACTS STRAIGHT

The Wassenaar Arrangement is an arms trade control group launched in 1996. Under its terms, most of the world's major arms-producing countries have agreed to declare any deliveries of conventional weapons to other countries. Like the United Nations register, the Wassenaar Arrangement covers weapons from big guns up to warships, but not small arms. After the terrorist attacks of September 2001, the USA persuaded some Wassenaar members to tighten their controls of small arms exports.

SOME TYPES OF SMALL ARMS *are more heavily regulated than others. During the last years of the 20th century there was a big campaign to limit the use of landmines. These weapons are often forgotten after a war, lying underneath the ground until someone treads on them. They cause horrible injuries and many deaths, often to civilians and children who may not realise how dangerous they are.*

AREA DENIAL

Landmines are one type of a group of weapons called Area Denial Weapons – they are designed to deny an enemy access to the area that has been mined. Early versions of mines were made of metal, which meant they were fairly easy to find with metal-detectors. Modern mines are made of plastic. They can be built to explode when trodden on (anti-personnel), or when a very heavy weight passes over them (anti-tank).

BANNING LANDMINES

A long campaign to ban anti-personnel landmines is finally having some success. Not all countries agree that all these landmines should be destroyed. Of the world's 193 countries, 146 have signed the 1997 Mine Ban Treaty. Since then, 22 million of the world's estimated 220 million anti-personnel mines have been destroyed. Even countries that are against a total ban, such as the USA, have destroyed some stocks of these weapons and limited their use.

Queen Noor of Jordan is one of many leading figures who actively support the campaign to ban landmines.

DIFFERENT NAME, JUST AS UGLY

Landmines are not the only way to achieve 'area denial'. In 1999, when NATO forces tried to restore order in Kosovo, warplanes dropped thousands of cluster bombs. These devices explode in mid-air, scattering hundreds of bomblets over the ground. Most bomblets explode, but the thousands that failed to do so in Kosovo were left for children and animals to stumble over. Cluster bombs are not banned.

➡ Unexploded cluster bombs can look like toys to children – but playing with them can cause serious injury and death.

FACING THE ISSUES

Landmines have claimed the lives of many people in the conflict between India and Pakistan over ownership of Kashmir.

- December 2001. Fears of war between India and Pakistan. Both sides lay up to three million mines along the border to prevent invasion by either side. Minefields are meant to carry warning signs, but many do not, and the majority of locals cannot read.

- January 2002. A woman and her child die in Kashmir after taking a shortcut through a field that has been mined.

- February 2002. Several civilians reported killed in Punjab.

- March 2002. Reports of up to 150 civilian deaths to date. The defence industry magazine *Jane's Defence Weekly* says that around 80 Indian soldiers have died in accidents while transporting or laying mines.

- Reports of casualties on the Pakistan side of the border are harder to find, though eight civilian deaths are known. Journalists in Pakistan are more limited in what they are allowed to report.

THERE ARE STRONG ARGUMENTS *for and against the arms trade. Governments have to find a balance between national security needs, the economic effects of buying or selling arms, and the ideal of peace. Different politicians have different answers to the problem, so arms companies, as well as campaigners against the arms trade, work hard to win politicians to their side.*

THE ARMS ARGUMENT

Arms makers try to make sure politicians and the public support their business. In the USA, the arms industry spends around $60 million each year on lobbying (paying expert campaigners to convince politicians to help them). Arms companies stress their role in creating jobs. Big arms-making projects in the USA are often spread across the country, so voters see a benefit to their local economy. For example, the multi-billion-dollar F-22 fighter jet has been built from parts made in 46 of America's 50 states.

⬇ *In 2000, engineers at the aerospace and arms manufacturer Boeing went on strike to demand higher wages. Arms firms argue that they provide many jobs.*

Demonstrators in Ukraine in 2003 protest against war with Iraq. Many peace campaigners argue that the arms trade fuels war.

Andrea Needham (left) and Joanna Wilson were two of the peace campaigners who attacked a Hawk jet in 1996. Their action was a protest against the sale of the plane to Indonesia.

AGAINST ARMS

There are several sorts of anti-arms trade organisations. Some work to advise international bodies, such as the United Nations, about problems arising from the arms trade – they may also suggest solutions to these problems. Some campaign to draw arms trading to the public's attention, where it can be embarrassing to politicians. These campaigns can force changes to national or international law.

UNILATERAL DISARMAMENT?

Some people argue that countries should stop buying and using weapons. When a nation gets rid of its arms without waiting for others to do the same, this is called unilateral disarmament. One country, Costa Rica, gave up its army in 1949 and has enjoyed peace ever since, despite conflict in other parts of Central America. However, a small nation like Costa Rica has far less to lose from unilateral disarmament than a larger nation, with allies who depend on it and potential enemies who might attack it.

FACING THE ISSUES

In 1996, a trial in the UK involved peace activists who had attacked a BAe Hawk jet with a hammer. The jet was due to be sold to Indonesia, which at the time was committing serious human rights abuses (see pages 22 and 24). The activists told the jury that they had a duty under international law to stop genocide by Indonesia. They argued that international law holds people responsible for a crime against humanity unless they did everything they could to stop it, even if that means breaking national laws. The jury found the activists 'not guilty'.

GLOSSARY

arms race: A race between two competitors to buy arms, to create the most powerful military force.

civil war: A war fought between two groups within a country.

Cold War: The conflict between the USA and its allies and the Soviet Union, which never quite tipped over into direct attacks. It started after the Second World War and ended in 1989, when the Soviet Union began to collapse.

coup: An attempt to take over a country, led by a group of plotters, often military leaders.

diplomacy: The working out of agreements and disagreements between countries through discussion.

dual use: Having a civilian use, such as medicine, as well as a possible use as a weapon.

exports: Products or services sold abroad, to another country.

Gulf War: The 1991 action by the USA and its United Nation allies to free Kuwait from occupation by Iraq.

human rights: Freedoms that should belong to all humans, such as the freedom from government brutality.

Iran-Iraq War: Between 1980 and 1989, a costly war fought between the bordering countries Iran and Iraq, which ended in stalemate.

landmines: Bombs designed to be left in an area and prevent enemy access. They explode when something touches the trigger.

military services: The work of skilled staff supporting an armed force, either by servicing equipment, training soldiers or providing reinforcements.

NATO: The North Atlantic Treaty Organisation, a military alliance of Western European and North American countries.

offset deal: A business agreement in which special extra benefits are won by the customer.

peacekeeping force: An armed force, normally neutral, which prevents rival armies attacking each other.

small arms: Infantry weapons such as guns, grenades, bazookas and shoulder-launched missiles.

social development: Improving the daily life of a society through advances in areas such as health, nutrition and education.

superpower: A nation with military and economic power far in excess of almost any possible rivals.

unilateral disarmament: Disposing of arms without waiting for other countries to agree to do the same.

United Nations: The international organisation established in 1945 to promote peace and cooperation between nations.

War on Terror: The name given to the series of measures taken by the USA and its allies in response to the terrorist attacks of September 11th 2001. These measures include the invasion of Afghanistan, as well as changes in national and international laws.

Wassenaar Agreement: The 1996 treaty that binds several states into a system which monitors arms sales.

Weapons of Mass Destruction: High-tech methods of causing massive numbers of deaths. They include nuclear, chemical and biological weapons.

FURTHER INFORMATION

MEDIA SITES

Defense News
This site provides news about the arms trade, including government policies and laws, new products and military strategies.
www.defensenews.com

Jane's
This site, from the publishers of *Jane's Defence Weekly*, includes information on military equipment, arms manufacturers and armies around the world.
www.janes.com

CAMPAIGNING GROUPS

Australian Campaign Against the Arms Trade (ACAAT)
ACAAT's website features a discussion forum and information on Australia's military expenditure.
www.acaat.org

Campaign Against the Arms Trade
The UK's main campaigning and lobby group against the arms trade.
www.caat.org.uk

Human Rights Watch
This site offers serious research resources, especially on arms that are borderline illegal, such as landmines and other area denial weapons.
www.hrw.org/arms

International Action Network on Small Arms
The International Action Network on Small Arms' website provides news on worldwide campaigns against the trade in small arms.
www.iansa.org

Landmine Survivors Network
The Landmine Survivors Network helps victims of landmines and raises awareness of their suffering. Its website contains many stories of people who have been injured by landmine explosions.
www.landminesurvivors.org

The Norwegian Initiative on Small Arms Transfers
Visit the fascinating Small Arms Transfer database to find out how much your country (or another one) is involved in the trade in small arms.
www.nisat.org

RESEARCH ORGANISATIONS

The Arms Trade Resource Center
This American organisation aims to educate people about the need to control the international arms trade. Its site contains reports, news articles and links to other websites.
www.worldpolicy.org/projects/arms

The Federation of American Scientists' Arms Sales Monitoring Project
This site is a good introduction to campaigns against the arms trade in the USA, and provides details of political influence as well as useful links.
www.fas.org/asmp

Stockholm International Peace Research Institute
This site provides information about the arms trade and how it is controlled, as well as peaceful ways to solve international conflicts.
www.sipri.se

MANUFACTURERS' ORGANISATIONS

The Defence Manufacturers' Association
The Defence Manufacturers' Association represents UK firms who make products for the defence industry.
www.the-dma.org.uk

The National Defense Industrial Association
The National Defense Industrial Association represents companies who supply military equipment to the US government. The association's website provides details of the relationship between arms firms and the US government.
www.ndia.org

INDEX